STREETLAMP NAUTILUS

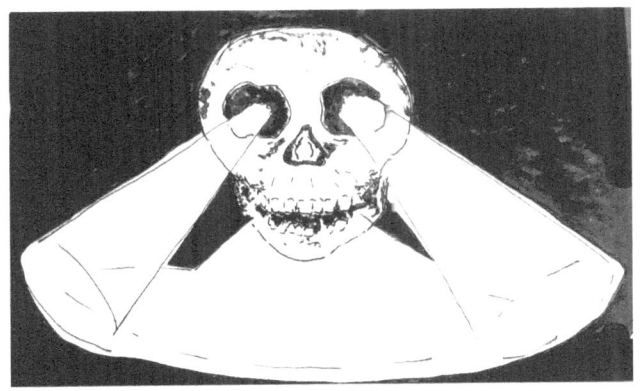

Poems by Catharine Batsios

Luchador Press
Big Tuna, TX

Copyright © Catharine Batsios, 2025
First Edition: 1 3 5 7 9 10 8 6 4 2
ISBN: 979-8-89975-021-2
LCCN: 2025946022

Author photo: Catharine Batsios
Cover image: Catharine Batsios
Dedication Image: Batsios Family Archive

Table of Contents:

Ackowledgments:

"Form of Collection," online, *Museum of Americana*, 2024,

"From Philly Doubletree to Independence Hall," 2022 print *PUNK* anthology, Kissing Dynamite Press,

"Kings & Queens in Collected Asterisms" is the June 2021 *Leavings*,

"Jellyfish Lesson" appears in *Glass Poetry*, August 2018,

"RE:Daedalus" was published by *Tinderbox* in December 2017,

Sections of "New York Prose Poem in Five Parts" appears in the inaugural issue of *GR8*, *a zine of art and literature*,

"Her" appears online, *Glass Poetry/Poets Resist*, 2017,

"My Mother on the Back of a Whale," *Linden Avenue Lit*, June 2017 (#61),

"Desire Wears Her Full-Metal Jacket," *Columbia: A Journal of Art and Literature* #51, 2016

"Form of Recollection" appears in *Chrysalism Press Issue 0*, Detroit 2025

A city is, in no particular order,
blood, and water, and smoke.

Streetlamp Nautilus
is the astigmatic halo which appears
during moments of perfect emptiness;
illuminates the golden ratio
                    of city
                              to blood
as they exist together, repeating.

Streetlamp Nautilus

Tom Z's Coney Island

was Lynette's last stand;
she had an aneurysm right there
behind the register, wanted to save time
& simultaneously get right through it
like the restaurant is the cup
& the light is at the bottom,
Coney Island stirred with cream.

Head-level bullet hole in a picture
window, vanishing point of a
last supper, a hole poked in membrane

> the outside place
> *theirs*
> the inside place
> *ours*

Tom Z's collects teenagers clunking
like hand-me-down Buicks
light in the tank.

Bodies made of light
stretch down to refuge in cracked vinyl seats,
light piled eight-deep,
light tripping, smoking light
pulling corners of the diner closer,
tucked light;
crescent wrench of evening
opens the valve of knife-fight night.

Desire Wears Her Full-Metal Jacket

Brass, they call it gliding metal
    malleable, doesn't spark, fends off particulate
   sounds like falling pebbles, or women

who used to wear coins
 chiming around their necks when they moved.
  Dowry of melodic polish,
     & like the last Buick to come off the line in
   Flint, MI—
necklace of rivets still glowing,
    city-hands fold the hood of a
    '96 LeSabre into a locket adding to the melody.

By night the chest of pistons and water pump
    cracks open, a raucous four city blocks of empty
      auto-shops come out all side-burns and
   beer tabs,
Chevy-in-the-hole sized smoke raking hair
as it dissipates, O *dowry of melodic polish*
   glass teeth striking from the parsed cavity,
     slick of machine grease lingering, never gone,
under nails, blackening down to the crescents.

Brass of deadbolt, of bullet—of full-metal jacket,
cold from being dipped in Gilkey Creek.
Gliding metal into evening,
tack-welded onto the rising moon.

Shark—Another Gliding Metal

Touch is a shark,
at first I latch onto her dorsal,
trail behind her like a soft parade of vermilion skin
and listen as we swim down Prentis
& Second. Was a time

when Touch was just something small,
couldn't reach both sides of a creek,
lingered between stones in the middle
while I counted stars wild enough
to show over traffic lights,
waiting for a tangle of creeping phlox
to make a carpet for the way home in the dark. Was
    a time

Touch was mercurial
taught me to keep a knife in my boot.
Touch taught me that when cut open,
my beloved will bleed streetlamps.
For my Birthday
Touch gave me an ID bracelet—*If found,*
please return to: The Streets.

Her skin makes music
like a metal drum

when she moves against the gravel
& here we are, on the corner
looking up. Touch has peeled
me like a wetted label on a
beer bottle—
Touch
has turned everything to water,
will be circling her chum
as I wade home in the dark.

Street Food/Requiem Shark

& you're guilty & grateful for gentrification,
(in Detroit, only a white body gets a streetlight)
you cross parking lots, sewer grates,
your shark/Saint of Touch sublimates when you look
directly into her—& you walk,
she brushes you as she passes,

on Prentis & Second you've made yourself a meal.
You marinate in the thought of night-coney coffee
paired with learning how to smoke, the bottomless eyes
you'd wait all night for, & used to, & still do
your requiem shark is thinking of hands full of hair,
the smell of paint, fresh blood on the sawblade.

You know that the best food comes from the back fat
of gas stations or liquor stores,
stewed meat the color of cinnabar,
served with flat bread,
blood moon
and lime

that spray and coat flavor to your skin,
burn your nailbeds in the places where
you've chewed thinking of Touch
& how you can avoid seeing her—
streetlight-astigmatism-mirage that she is—

requiem shark, your lost thought
who follows you home on nights
when city stars look more like white oleander.

What We Found in Those Nights

I held you between palms and sipped
the immediacy of black coffee,
swirling gestures with dark-roast eyes,
familiar like the steam from my cup.

In those diner-night escapades,
we were a temperature for gulping,
we were the casual refill,
we were the last drop.

Thalassophobia/Sirens

after Jamaal May

The clash of brass-haired Sirens only fills my streets
after water has been shed, & bodies
strewn; Siren song to accuse, to strip
from threads like Fates
snipping away inch by inch
until we have nothing left but stolen
moments & a confidence that future voice
is something other people use.

These Sirens
of toothy maw aren't fooling us,
not the bodies in which we have built our homes,
not even the injured or dead
who grow tired of waiting, blue-swaddled.
Sirens posture the shoreline
of names like North End or Southwest
purring, preening, sharpening, warming up,
& it isn't preference in music
that makes their cooing song
our face-down dirge;
Sirens of pyrite justice are simply a refrain
of the safety in your understanding
of the nature of the sea.

Record of a Flint Kid

33 1/3 after Wake Up Slow by Fernando Silverio Solis

Let's go out/just say when to leave/
this place don't mean what
   it used to mean

I watched leaves flip night yolk to silver
on the split limbs of wind, the smell of
asphalt, dirt, exhaust like some belly
dancer winding up from the expressway; blades
of grass nodding, I thought, *you'll never lose*
this tangle of green, the imprint of solitude on your skin
crawling moon as seen through rust at the alley fire escape.
Hear these, the delicate metals adorning that Flint smell
of highway & tires, a vigil of flammable ruts
not going home—at night I become leaves,
precious on the hip of the wind.

The place we met/burned down last week/
  it only exits now to you & to me

To a stranger my body might taste like a dive bar.
To a stranger my body might taste like a long drive.
To me my body is sour blood & just enough sleeping
in a Buick, to me my body tastes like *not quite*
or licking a battery, a fussy fuse box, a circuit popped
& yet to be reset—stretch like the back row movie theater,
like a mobius strip with a little extra each time around,
an empty lot with a solitary hoopty & one buzzing

light. My body is all of us in the back seat listening
to our song. A stranger might not like the taste of
my body, in my mind I understand but my tongue,
which is always tasting itself, does not.

I've been living in some kind of dream/where
nothing changes but me/it's the fear in
trying to leave

Drink the last drop of the sun before you go, come
January you'll wish you had it in you. When you're
always January, about to do something, inside your
car waiting for the frost to clear, drink the sun to melt
the cold. When you wake in who knows how many
Januarys bent like the window crank, something
about a car with manual windows will make you
feel insulated or in control—it's foggy & inconvenient.
In this iteration January's a brick wall in front & a
double parked car behind. You've spent your time
trying to press ash into light failing that, scuffing
boots to find a spark. Clutch in & easy,
you've learned to cut the wheel just in time.

My handful of seeds I put in the ground/
when it don't rain/only the foolish remain

Skeleton with pock-marks, I am a city
of loose bricks, hidden-in-this-picture,
fingertips touching, my whole self
a clandestine drop.

Clementines Instead of a Kiss Goodnight

In the neighborhood where Mom's car got stolen
    three times,
she rarely locked the door at night,
& only when parking lot was stark like black-box
S'agapo, koukla mou — did words present with one hand
cupping an incandescent citrus, the other foraging—

s'agapo, koukla mou, words, a present with
Child at the center, a tableau, Child climbing
on the table, Child of clementines appearing,
of hands that don't touch.

Only the muttering of shirtsleeves and workboots
in the leaving threshold—*S'agapo, koukla mou*—
as I turn on my heel to follow disappearing

Father as he turns on his heel to the rustle of
streetlights and sparse night-traffic;
the incandescence of us a certain tangle
with no human attributes.

I knew where he'd been when I saw clementines
on the kitchen table;
mesh torn the size of his hand— one for the road—I
could fit both of mine through the hole
& I picked a fruit from the crate.

In the neighborhood where I'd fall asleep listening,
playing *gunshot or fireworks?*
Mom still left the door unlocked for

Father, the scrim of shadow,
man who counts clementines as moments.
Child follows his trace out the door, off the porch, into
the pavement, then wet grass on stocking feet, my eyes
get lost between cars in the lot—
one hand cupping incandescent citrus, the other
    foraging.

Greek for *"I love you, my doll."*

Michigan Girl

For Hayes

I hear it said back to me in an earthy tone & I think
Seriously not another fucking pine tree image
or
some white girl at a bonfire wearing
an over-sized sweater/ she looks
wistfully at firespark rising into starscape.

O implicit ONLY, narrow
because the sign on the state line says
Pure Michigan;
I remember scrawling *Murder Mitten*
on every out-of-state bathroom for a year.

O, travel brochure ONLY of Hemmingway fly-
    fishing
and coming-of-age-as-a-frozen-river adolescence;
flintrock and kindling, plucked cherries at State Fairs,
living off of God's or Billy Durant's
paper-green land.

My Flint-spark was my platonic life partner and I
climbing over condemned concrete bridges
& every shoes
were the shoes that fit through chain-link,
remember those heels?

Remember those Chucks with the newspaper insoles
and how chips of stone and bird shit ruined
pairs of socks?

& that KEEP OUT. Of course there's danger
and yeah we could drown,
but we are already going there   what gaping

hole swallowing crows, rodents, flesh-rot
& Big Mac wrappers

let's not get sick from the Flint River
    we aren't drinking it like that yet.

Here's a joke: some 10ft-nothin' fence
could keep us out. Easily

we straddle the 1922 railing/36ft drop
into dirty-water rust and foam gurgle
of Hamilton Dam

but we got this

between you and the bridge
it was never the plummet
it was
I can't go home tonight
it was

right before birds start their pre-dawn racket
I'll meet you at the I-475 catwalk
back of the post office—

over by the high school we'l walk in the middle
of the road   of this hour like
potholes and faded lane lines—
an hour so empty you can lay in the road,
and you did
planted in the turn lane,
At least 6'2"
man, that's a big ONLY.

When Yr Grief Said Actual with a
Razor Tongue

Didn't you actually sit in the parking lot,
I passed through picket signs to the front desk—
We have your file, Miss, but require a password.
I said 'skippy' as if something like peanut butter
or the name of a family dog
would change its Actual.

There were four of us in the waiting room
soaking in actuality,
our eyes pitted by some booklets,
dismembered flesh, we read them.

I bought a drug store test
used it at the coney where all of us go,
our din of punk, hairclips, and cigarette smoke.
I slipped away, and when the women's room was
    occupied
Actual-event happened in the men's with the door
    locked—
it came in the form of a plus sign—so I threw the stick
away, buried it when I washed my hands, but it was still
there when I went back to the pile of used paper two
hours later.

Your tongue is sharp, you use it to cut away
what happened, like a doctor who counts back from ten
as anesthetic clouds a mind.

I actually was waking in a room that seemed like a
    birthing ward—
women in beds, attendants holding and guiding
to and from the bathroom where the trashcan was full,
I checked to see,

but Actual was somewhere else.
She left the room while I recovered,
passed you in the parking lot,
knew you wouldn't recognize her,

even now.

Re: Daedalus

The Mechanics of Flying (figs. 1-3)

It is said that burning sage
keeps restless spirits at peace.

Once a year for three days
Daedalus sits
under a mobile

crafted from the bones of a
sea bird

and watches the smoke
cling like feathers.

———

Two girls
were building a bridge
across a creek,

under a rock and covered in moss
like feathers
was the skeleton of a sea bird—

it couldn't fly.

———

On the third night,
     Daedalus had a dream
that a great dragonfly was upon his chest,

          "To fly, you must also be the wind.
     You know how to be the wind, don't you?
You just put your lips together and blow."

     When Daedalus woke from his dream he
   was very still.

On his chest was the perfect ash of a sage wand,
    he took a breath
        when he exhaled
           he became the wind.

The Story Doesn't End Until We See Icarus
   Again

Think of the sun as an eggshell,
and think that Icarus' descent—due to a trick of
light, and Daedalus' failing eyes—
was actually ascension.

In one acrobatic swoop,
  Icarus skipped like a rounded
      stone into the sun, gave it a
          good crack, and crawled inside.
Think of the embryo of a sea bird,
its molecular structure more
fluid and element than
sea-farer
or flight,

Think of the currents it created inside the shell
as its limbs, eyes and throat form
in mid-hatch
hesitation.

Think of its viscous wings
as it stills
and breathes,

of Icarus now,
being made of nothing but
salt
and feathers.

The Mechanics of Flying (fig. 4)

———

For your stemware,
you could use Daedalus' failing
eyes as coasters
when your not-quite steady
hand
pours slightly more
merlot
than you wanted.

The Second Coming of the Sun

Icarus hatched from the surface of the sun and seawater,
 had to teach himself how to breathe again—

> (he hadn't used his lungs since the
> fated moment when the pads of
> his feet left the tower; he will also
> argue that lack of oxygen and *not*
> hubris is why he was unable to
> stay in the sky.)

It wasn't until the hatchling's egg was gone
 and the basin of night filled
 that he remembered equal parts
 exhale
 and inhale

when he slept
it was the movement of water under his nose
that reminded him of the tether
of his father's beard.

Incubating Nymph Becomes Icarus Anisoptera

Famine at sea had made his eyes bulge
like ripe apricots,
his only consolation,

a fishing net that had freed itself,
bringing him fish scales, sea moss, the odd hook
or coin worn to a shine:

Icarus of salt and feather
had become Icarus of
crawling sea bed, Icarus of
his own weaving, Icarus of clove-hitch
or eye splice,

Icarus who spread his arms wide, whose
serendipitous net hardened as he brought it
out of the water across his back,

a dragonfly,

who in a surge of rapid-beating iridescence
became flight again.

The Physicist and Chemist on a
Motorcycle Tour

The town of Kalabaka comes off the tongue
like an olive pit you've sucked, it rolls off the plate
and leaves a deep red mark on the tablecloth.

The Physicist traces switch-back lines of mountain
roads on the map of Northern and Central Greece;
green for paved ones, brown for roads
that lead to monasteries.

The Chemist seeks out strangers to fill
extra shot glasses, mixes them with *Ouzo Barbayannis;*
he has stolen me from two tables over

asks me what being from Michigan
is like, I tell him
> *When traveling, you always wonder
> how close you are to fresh water,*

The Physicist works on space and time, a silver pencil
with fine lead, he draws from Kalabaka and circles
Agrini—
> *That was in my salad yesterday.*

In the viscous quiet forming in drops
of what's left at the bottom,

The Chemist pours another with ice cubes, watching
anise oil separate in plumes and cloud the glass,

> *He takes care of the travel, I drink the spirits,*
> *Barbayannis is Greek for water.*

Photo Albums of the Old Greeks were Roasted Peppers

Whose aroma filled the house even if they weren't
cooking right then. Men with rolled sleeves sitting
with women whose olive and gold necks from the
village broke waves and trimmed Buick sails to gather
in their restaurant's dining rooms in the evenings;

OPA!

Ripe, flecks of light like a bowl of strawberries sprinkled
with sugar from my Yaya's fingertips.

I take her hands which are wet and delicate and wrap
myself in the skin of roasted peppers

At the Restaurant, Sisyphus, Atlas, Prometheus

We work beside one-another,
Atlas is in the walk-in next to the eggs.
He comes out this time
with cabbages on his back, turns and
lets them roll into the processor.
    My Baba makes sure I've cleaned my arms
      up to the elbows
      before I pour dressing and shaved carrots
      into the bathtub-sized container.
      I pile and flatten the shredded planets
      until everything is coated in sheen.

From the kitchen to the basement,
there are 26 steps
one for each letter of the Latin alphabet
24 for Greek
if you skip the two that are rotting—
Greek sounds like water that is rambling,
enumerating, expectant of something.
I learned how to count from the sound
of the basement ice machine spitting cubes,
the simultaneous sound of Papou
clicking the komboloi
between his fingers in the office
      If I was lucky,
      If I was quiet,

I could crack the door, curiosity parting
cigarette smoke.
Basement of icons,
Holy Mother, Sacred Child poised
across from stacks of open ledgers
and produce invoices.
Carrying buckets
and buckets from basement to soft-drink machine;
    Alpha, Beta, Gamma,
  F-G-H-I, Theta
    Iota, Kappa,
        and down again,
Sisyphus has one hand in a bucket,
rattling cubes,
watching them leap over
the lip
        and down again.

The kitchen is chronic with flames, Prometheus,
who passed fire from Papou to Baba,
comes out to apologize
when Baba slams his fist onto the grill in frustration.
Prometheus wraps Baba's hand, this will happen
    again tomorrow.
When it's safe, Atlas brings out 5 more pounds
of meat, scrapes the charred pieces into the trash.
With his back to Baba, he will prep tomatoes,
    lettuce, onions as garnish,
then retreat
to his chilled domicile.

In winter the entrance and floors need to be kept clean.
Mud, salt, and melt pool while breakfast-eaters wait
to pick-up or cash out.

    Once an hour, Sisyphus taps me on the shoulder
     and says get to work.
    Girl-child and mop handle which stands 14-inches
       above
     her crown, bucket of water spilling
     from tile to carpet
     Baba watches
     satisfied
     from his fire-trench of double-cheeseburgers
     and three-egg omelettes.
    Papou emerges to put money in the till
    sees my small mass in muddled water
    treads out to me and even with an arthritic neck
    prefers to do the job.

If I'm lucky, if I'm quiet, I get to watch with a straight
    back,
full chest as the old man
puts Sisyphus, Prometheus to shame.

Prometheus whispers in Baba's ear when this happens.
He comes out front
without words but with flames for me and
for Papou, his father,
It's the girl's job he says, *not the old man's.*

Papou's mouth opens into a freshwater lake, remembers
the village, remembers the water and human skin
between then and now,

My eyes are a freshwater lake as Prometheus whispers,
fanning the flames in Baba's tone,

Papou is high tide, good fishing, calm day. Prometheus
has no currency here, returns to his place
of hot oil and gas flame.

Eggs/Potatoes/Toast

Yaya's Restaurant Work

—

Hashbrowns on porcelain
she peeled potatoes all day;
I fill, her hands ache.

—

Baba

—

Cooked egg yolks pool, smear
you taught me dip, soak with toast.
The yolk starts open.

—

Papou's coat was soft
you wear it after his death,
missed the funeral.

—

Papou was bread at
heart, head down immigrant, cook,
he breaks, I am full.

—

Comfort Food

—

Child made of porcelain
born unchipped, washed, for cradling
eggs/potatoes/toast.

Legacy

It's when I'm putting on makeup. I see her
     fingertips
applying powder on creases and brows. Not me
at the mirror, I'm a three-year-old, frilly socks,

5:30 a.m. awake for the opening shift—then light
in the pockets as I tie apron strings behind me.

I sit at Theio's diner on my own time, my own
     coffee
stains on white oxford, eggs, potatoes, toast,
     ordered

in verbal shorthand: 2OE/HB crisp/WW shake
ten hours of restaurant shift from my hair.

I shoot pool left handed because she taught me
in her form. I take whiskey in sizable drinks, wince,

tilt my head like she did the first time she caught
     me with
a glass in hand. Going home now would be
     resignation.

She puts near-military creases in my uniform for
     tomorrow,
I argue but take a bath anyway. I like brushing my
     teeth now.

She diminishes, nestled on top of laundry
instead of mattress. Diminishes, but not before

she counts the change in her pocket, stacks it
beside me. Loose metal, rounded dollars on reserve,
small pleasures larger in certain hands.

Desire Walks at Night on Saginaw St.

Flint, spark, river, bed, light-playing trace
on backbone, city bricks
are the tide silting
    boulevard glide jostles clamped shells
     to reveal pearl of light elongating
    buildings of dark silver and moss—
  water-memorized safe passage through the condemned
stairwell of the long-abandoned hotel;
pieces of chitin scratched off and sinking.

        Chitin—from Greek for a soldier's tunic—the
        naturally formed shell, exoskeleton on living
          creatures;
        Flint—a mineral formed from crustaceans, or
        other living animals which use *chitin* to clothe
          themselves.

When snaps of light occur, it's because Flint,
   the harder of two
striking surfaces, breaks off pieces
and ignites in a halo

of *chitin* and crackle,
bioluminescent trails
    where Touch has been,
     opening the chest to current and surface tension—

Desire is like dropping an egg from a few stories up,
  forward three somersault pike, traffic pattern,
      metallic
    city night sound—brass chorus as she performs
     immersion. Expect she will sleep
      in the orange yolk of morning.

Thalassophobia/Fear of the Sea

After Jamaal May

I think of the bodies of the people I've loved
as we are a sameness/one drop
in the sea/containing the whole sea
the sound of hands through hair is the far-off
wave, low tide of forehead I welcome
to my breast.
I fear for the bodies that I have loved,
bioluminescence mutated out of necessity
for lifetimes without light
for all the caverns we are,
for the Giant Squid Greed wrapping its entire self
around the good days, leaving a mark like
told you so, or *never out of reach*.

All the bodies I've loved look for a messages in bottles
they/we make notes and carry them
we are touch without thinking the word
before the event, implicitly
we are the feeling of one-another
our bodies pulled across the horizon/un-happened.

Eight arms of suction paralysis
can tell you that the bodies I've loved
show concentric circles of
*just until the end of the day, just until
the work is done, just until*
is the call of Giant Squid Greed;

low utterance under scar tissue,
skin healed over and swimming away.
Giant Squid Greed blossoms under ridges

like some monstrous chrysanthemum
then converges, tentacle-weave steeling
what little light travels to where we dive so deep.

I fear for the bodies I've loved, which does not
    include
my body, living.

The Feel of Cold and Cigarettes

Standing in the entrance, I saw that the light in your room was red and you sat brooding under it. A few steps in, I remember the way walls showed everything that we did there—whether it was a dent from moving in, the cracked stains of beer bottles being launched from the couch, the smell of your smoke, flumes of lost conversations or the constant reverberation of music that lingered—like fingerprints from unwashed hands.

I walked to the crooked-frame window of your dilapidated hut; being above ground and going below, down the stairs outside of your half-basement apartment. I followed the sidewalk to the dead end where all the leaves collected to hide from winter claws.

It was the feel of cold and cigarettes cutting off my breath before I could completely take it in.

Ode to Leaves Growing into the Window, July 2007 or With All These Leaves, I Finally Figured You Out

It was the summer of 113 ½ Louis Street—

Summer of longing for my friend who left to
study in Mexico, summer of crawling through the
window and shrubs to work at the gas station on the
other side, summer

of duct taping blue scarves on the ceiling to cool
the room, summer of falling asleep in dampness,
summer of waking

at night when light from the gas station combed
through, pushing green bark spindles through a
missing pane,

summer of drifting off with leaves

on my skin, I thought a greeting from Monterrey,
instead of you—

Summer of car-living when the lease was up, summer
of prying the metal spatula into the back door of the
house in order to shower then crawl through the
window to work, summer of fat rain, summer
of cracked window seals,

the summer that, even though I wasn't yet yours, you
drove eighty-nine and a half miles to help me move my
things that had finally been thrown on the curb,
summer of dampness, of blue-eyed waiting

as we sat together one last night,

the summer of night-growing leaves which I might
    still find
tangled in your beard.

October Night in a Bottle

It's about boot heels for metronomes tonight,
the out of tune guitar grinning on the upstroke
is our Harvest, is our reveling
in daybreak frost never coming—

can be
warded off
by rosy cheeks
a two-step
a whisky breakdown—

not yet, not yet.

Drinking off cold to keep a rhythm
in step with Michigan months
shifting to auburn tones
like old newspapers
piling under the basement steps,

until booze hounds trickle into blankets,
incubate into hangovers
thrown on living room couches,
floors, acres,

the cuddled up crop
of open mouths snoring
sleeping off the reasons we drink,
the Harvest Gathering.

If It were Bourbon Instead of an Apple

Nakedness,
   a broken ring,
      the back porch and
tree cover around us—

When I told the story of the first time I
finished a bottle of bourbon myself,
Marianne said "…no shame, a reversal of
Adam and Eve."

The same night that whiskey put me to bed—
   I came back naked in the kitchen arch—
was the night that Jo, slapping the side of the house in
time with the guitar
broke her ring

on the upstroke. Jo beat at the silver-plated band,
  beat at
cracks until the metal let go
fell into a puddle of beer under the table:
    my body in the yellow of the kitchen arch, my
       hair washed with whiskey sweat and
       cigarettes, my body
       uncovered,
  my body swaying with drunk-delayed equilibrium
came in on the downstroke. She gave me a bottle
  and we drank,

letting fingers of our smoke
        clasp

            and

                break

concentric shapes of back-porch Eden, shapes of
   October
 evening carrying on,
letting rings of blue
          daybreak,
             rings of glasses sweating,
          rings of empty bottles,
        rings of used filters—

a ring of sun, nakedness, a broken ring

From Philly Doubletree to Independence Hall

Started at night, bodies alight under
hotel marquee/rendezvous/leaving arm in arm/
Desire and her Jersey Socialists/
　bodies of
　　　bourbon flush,
　　　　lit-like-Hopper parking ramps,
　　　　　hours of cast-metal silence
　/bodies of light/
　　re-arranging nightfall
　　　six pair/oxblood kicking/
　　　　so much pavement.

Hang left when buildings shift mosaic
/arrive/boots like skin stained red/
　broken glass/
　burst like dahlia bloom,
　　maybe fireworks/

Wasn't open/Independence Hall/couldn't
accommodate the rasping panel's interrogation
/coming into dawn/red-boot aubade/six-part
　　breakdown
of
　pale,
　　unapologetic
　　　　fathers/

Lunar Cycle/Full Red Moon

I lived in her twice,
Betty was her name, after
my mother who hates what her
middle initial stands for,
my oxidized, clay colored Betty
'92 LeSabre whom I inherited
when YaYa got her new Malibu and I got
promoted from the middle of the backseat
to the captain's chair.

In these summers, we are merchants of
abstraction. A trade route plotted from one all-night
diner to the next, exchanging secrets from the four-
    corner booths for coffee, tea, and gold
french fries.

Gummed up fuel injectors—
one foot on the brake, one foot on the
accelerator at all times—to cradle her
momentum at red lights, she needs a constant
influx of gas
and so we lie waking,
incubate
behind the dive bar as neon vines
grow through the door seals, weave into upholstery,
    blanket of
August-midnight tallow covers us both,
to sweat off in the morning.

I use my sight of night-creepers winding
to recall a modest cargo:

        two pressed uniforms in the trunk, a few
        summer skirts, painted jeans and sandals
        from freshman year, sketchbook riding shotgun,
        Rebetika mix tape in the deck, it reminds me
          of distance
        from first birth to now
        under sky passing
           with one broken tail light.

Untitled Red Poem

i.

Like the smell of
old books, night-shade sidewalk
red soaked from the bar district;

a color in the back of your mind as you
held your glass and insisted on filling mine,

we are two volumes,
shelved side by side, or
read in mouthed words;
                    half-held on your tongue.

ii.

"you say 'oh my god' a lot during sex."

He looked at her in the backdrop of walls dingy
    with cigarettes and water stains,

"I've been described with a great many words…"
She picked up her pack from the floor, shook it
    to find the lighter,
opened the box and took her favorite cigarette.

There was red in her nails as she brought the rolled
    paper to her mouth,

 "…but *pious* was never one of them."

iii.

you course with red;
coarse with red from my fingertips,
red from my mouth

Five Nights a Week

I am a woman, self-aware
making a point with a slurred speech
on Modern Feminism
while I stagger the same three feet
in my blue jeans and bra.

I am a French Impressionist painting,
naked in a winter hot tub drinking wine
smiling pretentiously
through rambling steam.

I am a lounge singer
half-cocked on the couch
at 4 a.m.crooning on about
my broken sequined heart.

I'm a jilt, a shrug,
a couple bats of the lash,
a renaissance of expertise, but mostly,
I'm a bottle of booze
come closer, darling,
we'll lose ourselves in
my own drunken rant.

Another Reason Not to Keep Spares

Keys, Wallet, Chapstick,
Lighter, in the jeans.

Pack, extra Pack, Phone,
Gloves—both of them—
51 cents, in the jacket.

Dignity,
Grit.
.

Everything I've ever lost is in my pockets.

Cigarette Break on South Side

Living here is only living at night, catch
the last train to the last bus wait in vapor
after second shift
there is a coffee shop with a shot and a
    sidewalk—

the city whose rhythm I found like some idiot
savant of late hours and neon signs, air
damp, greedy with hands on the sides of my neck,
behind my arms, small of my back
I don't ask it to stop,

I don't ask Pittsburgh to stop touching me like this.

I ask about my Stoop-Sister who
wrote a diary full of letters to Paulie
while we laid in bed and watched
Mary Tyler Moore on her smartphone,
why did she mourn a man we only met
because it was midnight on Easter Sunday
and we were rolling a joint
on the church steps next door—

I ask why Paulie walked along
Brereton street, up and down the double yellow line,
he said it was the only way to travel,
said he was on the edge of the Earth.

I ask about Carlene at the opposite platform,
Red Line to make it home,
who called me not 'Love' but 'a Love'
and wished us both a happy early birthday
before she vanished.

I ask why I can never, ever, for two states now,
hold on to my left glove for more than a week,
I ask where to find the perfect cup of terrible coffee
to warm my left hand,

I ask about the Red Theater,
about that game we play called
'give it a name'
and I wonder if I'll ever be able to name anything,

I ask until atmospheric pressure
is a migraine,
damp hands clench into downpour—
under the slick of
rain-dripping-fry-grease from my skin
the pavement is strung
like a strand of prayer flags.

Gilded Day has Leaked

6 p.m. is for galvanized steel as L & I wrestle it from
    the ground:
3rd & Stevens will never be the same.
10 foot pole with the street signs still attached
hangs out the back of the car, the car that hits a
    pothole
and sings Hallelujah,
by 8 p.m. gilded day is running on

window panes. Saginaw St. is a corridor of sunset/
& our petty crime turns into pay it forward as
we tap 1-9-8-6 into the keypad of B's apartment
    building/
leave 3rd & Stevens in the laundry room
on the table called "FREE to Take"

and drive away. When she came home,
    B cussed us out
to her basket of work shirts, sat next to 3rd &
    Stevens &
let the wash do its thing.

My Mother on the Back of a Whale

She said
       "Baby, do your thing."

My mother has always wanted to see the backs
        of whales break the ocean, to watch their
        flukes the size of a few humans submerge
        like nothing happened.

This is how I think of her most. Not all those years
        we spent landlocked in low-income housing.
        Not all those boxes I unpacked when she
        wasn't looking—old track medals; she was
        very good with her feet on the ground
        and running,

she quieted her feet only to say
       "Baby, do your thing."

        And I left her behind when we both
        couldn't go and see things
        she's only read about.

        I drank silt-bottom coffee at alley tables
        somewhere near a fountain in Rome,
        I dug up corroded drachmas from sand
        on an island not far from my father's birth,

in sleep between days of restaurant work, I
imagine she runs barefoot on the back of a whale,
the slippery landmass breaking water.

"Baby, do your thing."

Form of Recollection

It has something to do with the time of day, evening,
what we call dusk,   but I call blue time.

I watch anglerfish—they below who crease sidewalks,
cigarette embers leading them toe-tap to toe-tap,
anonymous night sounds mark
Fibonacci sequences of a city.
The thrall of orange edging out/invasion of cobalt
     shard
settles on our uneven planes,
     up the brick ripple of Saginaw St.,
          down the urchin spines of Woodward Ave.,
through the lit aquaria of half-basement apartment—
into the flint spark/revelation of a tide pool:
a handful of broken granite, a loose brick, saplings
     grown from between cracks, empty 5 a.m. parking
     lots, beams embossed like
sheet metal come from the moon and make a ghost
     ship tableau.
My chest is an ocean floor for these things collecting.

I've bathed well in the glow of tourmaline love,
jewels dropped down to sink and light the way,
I've learned how to wring night air into a tall glass
for a toast.

It has something to do with sweating on your sheets
around midnight,
a muslin layer of wax on the skin
catching a glint from skyward artifacts;
the vertebrae of Ursa Major aligned point north—
a brown bear in a tributary who claws gleaming trout
from under my sunken trees and river stone,
Aquila skims me trying to attract my creatures
to the surface—I blow a puff of smoke into his feathers
and watch him retreat into mercurial tint of insomnia.

I keep a snapshot of you hidden like treasure.
You, at the mouth of a cavern
gasp of light which makes you only a
dim shape/dark contrast/ those nights
we stood on our ghost ship/and called our city
    Atlantis—

It's vertigo from the sloping roof of timeline,
    a barracuda
fixated on the horizon glint,   my high tide,
the blue time.

Jellyfish Lesson

Think of Turritopsis dohrnii which starts its life cycle
anew when mortally threatened

Translucent like the water in which you were born,
its body, the shape of tide/
mimic of the space around you—

feel it when it comes close to ask
why you didn't know she had bruises
under her raglan cotton sleeves—
how you couldn't tell she was washed

in three years of silence,
how were you so into yourself that you didn't feel
her arm tense when you took it—
genial until membrane sting,

that jellyfish question.

At first, when it comes close
you don't even think there is a question
billowing grotesque in safe waters
& you remember the jellyfish found off the coast
in the Mediterranean,
how when it dies
cells escape its body, & it's young again

not unlike your mothers being hunted
& trapped under dressers as children, or

other stories of cooking grease, teeth,
tufts of hair missing in pigtails,
a legacy of hiding in the yard while a woman
was at the jellyfish end of a sawed-off shotgun.

It crept inside when you were a girl and
you answered with nights slept in cars
or diners, or waiting,
answered with smoke, your own ugly body
that hasn't deserved one good thing ever.

But just now it comes close,
& you feel something leave your bodies
as you share a doughnut
& she washes
three years of silence down with milk.

New York Prose Poem in Five Parts

I. Almost

The air in Murray Hill is——. You can see individual drops, but they never quite make it to the ground. On Lex and 38th some Australian tourists are looking for 8th Ave, and you tell them to go west; the numbers get smaller toward the East River until they're just a bike trail of chewing gum and bird shit. Murray Hill stays on your skin as you leave a wake from the corner to the bagel shop. Just the bagels, please, don't say shmear, you'll get farmer cheese at the market/ opened at 7am, you were already on the train from Harlem by then. 9 mos in the city, without a job, with insomnia, and the feeling of *almost* every time the city gives you something like the air——, and traffic is slow, stop-motion, you would think delirium if it weren't for the smoke you turn into animals of white and gone. One foot out the door, *almost,* your books are already packed, almost, you have a room in Detroit when you want it, *almost*, but the air in Murray Hill is so big.

II. Warm Weather

There are black sequins in the closet, A-line impulse buy from shoulder-stitch to hem you just wanted to fit into this city, rather wanted this city to look good on you, for once. It does. In August some journalist prowling Union Square took your picture 'cause your style was on point. The camera was so uncomfortable because he's chatting and you talk with your hands and extra chins don't look at the tooth gap and coffee stains. Warm weather means you spend a few weeks thinking about people on the train looking at your

leg hair and being disappointed every time you pass
a window or a mirror that calls you out on meaty
shoulders but you don't shave, and don't have
room in your head to think about sweat stains in 80
degree weather. It's only February, though. You were
supposed to have more time to make it before the
grass in Union Square was for sitting again, you were
supposed to have it together enough to be one of
those bad bitches wearing heels in Manhattan, you
even bought the teal lipstick for those black sequins
in the closet, but scuffed Docs and pocket change
for a cup of tea will have to do.

III. Snake Mistakes

You like it when you walk down Houston between
1st and 2nd where New York forgets to be New
York and missing Detroit doesn't seem like a snake
slithering into its old skin. Your skin used to be
cracked tar and potholes and Detroit diamonds
and it was breezy like a highway overpass. This city
tries to fill you in without consent, some SoHo
restoration, faux-noir, drink-your-rent-money-
with-a-twist-of -lime kind of fill you in but today
someone at the Mercury Lounge soundcheck was
tugging at his beard like how you tug at the sidewalk
when you don't want New York to be New York you
remember how good you and your boots have it and
something like affection slithered right into you.

IV. More Tigers

She gave you a rough-cut turquoise pendant, and
someone else gave you those amber, glass, and
black/ochre painted beads so you made a necklace.
It wraps around your neck three times, and you feel
powerful like when you heard the old-school poet
say that Scorpio women should wear amber to

balance their energy, like the time you made it in the downpour from the train station to the liquor store to fix your hair in the reflection of the cooler just before he drove by to pick you up, like the time you hung out the passenger window going down the highway to pull debris caught on the antennae: someone steadied you, wrapped three fingers around your ankle, you were beautiful and dangerous.

V. The Metrograph

The theater is something well-designed and thoughtful. On [Ludlow and Canal] if it weren't for a black awning with art deco lettering, you wouldn't know it was there; the rest of the block is NO PARKING/brick/metal/ graffiti. Inside, you're greeted by a smallish woman with horn-rimmed glasses and a necktie, she's selling tickets. There is a bar, a waiting area with french-style sofas and mismatching end tables. You look around. The whole thing feels very sparse, contemporary & post-war, like maybe the proprietors found the original furniture in the basement and brought it out so that the silver dessert cart will get some use again, it displays movie theater candy. If you are too cagey to stay downstairs, or curious, or hungry, you can ascend to a mezzanine lobby which has a full bar, limited seating for breakfast lunch or dinner, a reading nook where you browse and buy something written about film. There are tables and antique mirrors & you think you've seen this Ingrid Bergman backdrop. At some point, a woman with a tea-tray filled with candles will come by and put a light on your table. The room will dim as you finish your drink. When it's time to catch the show, you turn a corner, go through a discreet door into a black vestibule lit with a single desk lamp on the floor, a single floor-length mirror leaning against the wall.

Her

There's a woman who owns a junk shop
& when there's a loose tile in the foyer,
a piece of glass that looks like Flint, she yelps.
These cold crackle fragments rest
in the tension of her palm;
old guitar strings woven into a necklace,
Virgin icon from the rear-view of the Buick she slept in,
empty clementine crates storing spices & cups
for Greek coffee, Dalmatian shells from a far off coast,
snapshots of dirt & river water.

Some days she's the kind of woman who,
while she reads poetry in the afternoon,
hires an artist of the tongue to perform
cunnilingus.
Other days she puts on a leather jacket, climbs
into running bathwater because she's lonely
& imagines that's how she came out of the womb.
But really, no womb would ever have her,
her gaze moves around my apartment twitching;
the fridge kicking in, pieces of Carrera quarry
shifting in an ashtray; she smells like cinnamon from
    Sullivan St.
& cleans her teeth with an X-acto knife.

I want to hit her with the brick from a Pittsburgh street
I lived on once, tuck her into a cigar box, arrange her
like a musicbox ballerina, pin her up with cast-iron
    nails
pulled from a 19th-century church,
or maybe ask her out for beers at some Bowery
    basement bar
where she'll only order Michigan brews, one Two-
    Hearted
after another.

She is the one of us who still has paint in her hair,
she still has that pair of jeans I wore backstage,
& never left the roof of the Durant Hotel that night
when we broke in to see the lights down Saginaw St.
Her junk shop is somewhere near the Flint River
where she catalogues, cleans & tells stories to her
    trinkets
so I can hear stories again
in that foreign tone someone who has never been a
    lover uses.

She Goes In Head First

Drip of alley overhang
fire escape, the cold
metal
where in the warm months
a body made of nightshade
kissed the back of her neck;

Desire counts her age in icicles,
melts from exhaust at the intersection
dirt and snow slide down her face.
At the hour of perfect emptiness—
to hear thick snow-tread tires on the street—
the whole city-block vibrates.

Desire pries back plywood

walks down a rusted-out stairway

what would have been a basement
is now scratch of winter
graffiti sprawl of frost

Desire folds her body
into the shape of last light
ignites her palms on char from a trashcan fire

she considers
everyone outside the city limits
who say that Downtown
this time of
night
is the tip of a knife or
a hand muffling the mouth.

Sometimes it is.

Solitude on this occasion is soft
and airy
sweet
but not too

she eats herself whole.

Kings and Queens in Collected Asterisms

*"A wound gives off its own light
surgeons say."*
      --Anne Carson

Starmap: Allentown, PA

At the Starlite Diner—coordinates 233 Pennsylvania
      100—you see
the *King of Cups*, a constellation appearing
in the tabletop horizon at late dawn
after an ice storm. If you
arc between two spots of light
which are a glint on the gold of
wire frame glasses,
you have found the pointer stars.
You may miss them

if you don't drink enough coffee, if you doze on cold
      vinyl waiting
for your pancakes to arrive, or go out
to pace the gravel with your third cigarette.
If you aren't careful or still, glare from the 6:17 a.m.
      sun
will obscure the light cluster called *Butter Knife*
poised over a smattering of hot sauce on egg.

John's meticulous dissection
is how we explain the perfectly quadrilateral sections

of the *Broccoli and Swiss Omelette,*
a nebula just below the elbow.

Also visible, the blue planet which makes up
the right iris—it gazes in the direction of the *Queen of
   Cups,*
rising eventually in the next months, stretching her
   arms against
the backdrop
of the eastern sky.

Inquiry into Asterisms (1)

It is only through association that we mention the
King of Swords.

Picture a man who balances stars on an absinthe
spoon to cut bitter wormwood, who then thinks he
is elevated, hallucinates that he is made of light,

how the mind can perform contradiction, fool itself
into believing that above and below can feel the same.

**Introduction to the King of Swords/
An Illusion Involving Pieces like the Moon
as the Buttons on a Three-Piece Suit**

Being a scientist, you found a way to hold a constellation
between your thumb and forefinger, keep it as the
     moving gears
of the watch in your vest.
Because she saw a horn-rimmed moon in the buttons
     of your
waistcoat, the *Queen* thought she was still in the orrery
     of night
even when you touched her under lamplight in the
     street, or when
she stood on the sill, back arching, arms behind her,
fulcrum of your palm.

Not being from a place this far north, you've kneaded
     your hands
to disguise how cold they were—the *Queen*, your
     object, was
narcissistic to think that you were her overcoat
in early spring frost,
that you were anything but a blade across her
     shoulders,
still chilled from winter,
King of Swords. King of nothing more
than precision, but king of the affectation supine
in her, *Queen of Cups*. Queen of bourbon nights, or
the shapes of her asterisms,

points of interest, intersection, points along the spine,
the vertebrae you've found to render her motionless,
to take her out, just to check the time.

Inquiry into Asterisms (2)

Our protagonist, the *King of Cups*, is patient, has learned
    equally
the head and the heart, doesn't presume to hold an
    orrery in the
palm—insists that they are only a piece of it, and
    therefore
cannot contain the whole outside of itself.

They are also the only fixed grouping
in the *Royal Constellation Cluster*. Quite literally, the
Queen makes a path around them
taking in every perspective
over time.

Kings and Queens Leaving Footprints

I.

The *Queen of Cups* is a constellation showing the end
    of winter,
I am visible only once I take off my shoes,
once I go into the new grass and pull petals from
the Scarlet Beebalms, throw them toward the night sky
to make a portrait;

we leave footprints, not like dancers or orienteers, but
    light-footed
like glass on a string, or waiting
between reflection
and constellation.

II.

I wish his socks would not leave footprints on the wall
as the *King of Swords* sits there, reversed, on my couch.

He looks at me like a shard of glass tied on a string
    held to light.
I look at the things he left for me
tracing a slender heel
and high arch
walking toward me.

The *King of Swords* places his blade between us
on the wooden floor, he expects me to
hold up my skirt,
step lightly on either side.

The barefoot *Queen of Cups* chooses instead
to let him cut open her feet,
she chooses stop-motion dawn,
trails petals from her wounds as she leaves.

Final Inquiry into Asterisms

Queen beside the *King of Cups*, queen of bourbon
    nights, of blue
hours, with petals trailing from her feet across the sky,
queen of the cup with a pinhole, queen of parking
lots, of bus stops with bright moon overhead, queen
of grass wet from blood, queen of stop-motion dawn,
queen of the bottomless cup.

Form of Collection

Before I pay *cash only*
for my royal blue driving gloves,
some soldier named *Harry's* Zippo
from 1943, and that glass ashtray
large enough to be a gravy boat,
I look at buttons in jars—
lidless jars at Eastern Market, buttons
light in my hands, cupping fingers like
pistachio shells, giving me
one last chance
to take them home. They've accumulated there,

They are shaped like the ones from inside great-
    grandma's hall closet,
the buttons in the sugar tin next to the pens with
    licked nubs,

They are shaped like a honeycomb in the center
where I've stored things like great-grandma's brooches
from the Hudson's catalogue with missing gems,
her back bedroom with the sewing machine
where she taught me to take three steps and twirl,
where my foot slipped, and bobbin's thread went
    through fabric
into my ring finger.

They are shaped out of bone
with glass in the middle like my mother
at the kitchen table in her bathrobe,
head in hands after the first time
she slapped me for telling her no.

I take out the mother
of pearl and set them aside.
I take out the brass ones sealed with foreign alphabet;
they smell like sweat and onions from my father,
and perfume from my shampoo
when I hid them under my pillow to translate them.

I take out the red ones that hit the light like tiger's eye
and move them under my tongue and bite down,
drawing blood to hide them
for later—

in my room by light siphoned through blinds, one
    by one
I take them out—the blood eye and the tiger's eye—
fasten them to the front of my coat for safe keeping.

Evening Runs Out

Coney at 3 a.m. when the kid who talks like Walter Cronkite breaks the coffee-jitter silence and says *follow me I know what we can do.* He gets into his '93 Ford with the tailgate like a tongue, more get into the Buick leave open-mouth rubber in the parking lot. Evening clenches shut following tail lights at 90 m.p.h./speed limit 45. Walter Cronkite drives the morning news right back to where it started, where we eat breakfast before school, where we forgot to pay.

To Diane Wakoski, who taught me how to build from light, to Robert Turney, mage of fire, creeping water vines, & Christmas lights, to Diane's table, every one of these poems was passed over it & the hands it contains, specifically Anna Newman, Korey Hurni, Justin Groppuso-Cook.

To everyone helping me grow my craft & literary comraderie.

To my city. Shoutout to Flint Local 432 for keeping me alive—support yr local venue.

Catharine Batsios is from Flint, MI & has
lived in Detroit since 2013 as a practicing
artist, teaching artist, & literary community
organizer.

This project was made possible, in part, by generous support from the Osage Arts Community.

Osage Arts Community provides temporary time, space and support for the creation of new artistic works in a retreat format, serving creative people of all kinds — visual artists, composers, poets, fiction and nonfiction writers. Located on a 152-acre farm in an isolated rural mountainside setting in Central Missouri and bordered by ¾ of a mile of the Gasconade River, OAC provides residencies to those working alone, as well as welcoming collaborative teams, offering living space and workspace in a country environment to emerging and mid-career artists. For more information, visit us at www.osageac.org

Osage Arts Community